MAMMOTH MAGIC

Story written by Shelley Gill
and
Illustrated by Shannon Cartwright

MAMMOTH MAGIC
ISBN 0-934007-01-2
PAWS IV PUBLISHING
P. O. Box 2364
Homer, Alaska 99603
Copyright 1986 ©

First edition 1986
Second edition 1988

Library of Congress catalog number
86-090425

Dedicated to
My grandmother, Esther Schaubel, who experienced
the arctic nights 40 years ago.
S.C.

And to Gabe, who loved the night and me.

S.G.

Above the village an early winter sun rode across the mountain tops. Inside one of the small wooden houses a young Eskimo boy traced icy designs on his frosty bedroom window.

Today was the first day of the winter caribou hunt and the men were busy loading gear and rifles on the snowmachines. But Andy was not going on the hunt.

He had made his decision the night before and now, as he sat on the edge of his bed, a tear rolled down his brown cheek.

It wasn't the cold or the loud noise of the guns that scared him. Or even the wolves that chased silently behind the herd. Andy's fear was a simple matter.

He was afraid of the dark.

During the early days of arctic winter, if he climbed the hill behind his house, he could see the great icepack of the Bering Sea. His village, called Eklok, was surrounded by stunted spruce trees and he loved to watch the sun glint off the icicles that hung from the craggy branches. But the winter sun was gone too soon for Andy. In Eklok, when the snows came, the sun only lifted above the horizon for a few hours each day. The rest of the time it was dark and Andy was afraid of the things that lurked in the nighttime shadows.

There was a knock and Andy's big brother, Rudy, stood in the doorway.

"Are you sure you won't change your mind and go with us? You could carry the flashlight," he offered.

"No," said Andy quietly. Rudy shrugged his shoulders and turned away. A few minutes later Andy heard the roar of the snowmachines and the hunting party was gone.

Andy just sat and stared out the window. He wanted to be brave. But just the thought of spending all those nights out on the trail made him shudder.

A small sound caused him to turn. Tobuk, Andy's grandfather, was lifting a pack on to his back. He smiled at Andy. "You want to check traps with me?" he asked.

"Sure," said Andy and he grabbed his parka and together they headed for the low ridge where Tobuk's snares were set.

As they crunched through the thin crust of snow Tobuk pointed out the signs of the changing seasons to his grandson. Andy was startled when a ptarmigan abruptly exploded from the willows in a flurry of brown and white flapping. "See how the hen is nearly white now?" Tobuk said. "As the days grow short she trades her brown summer colors for white, just like the fox and the hare."

"What do you mean?" Andy asked.

The snow was falling gently as Tobuk stood looking toward the brush where the bird had landed.

"Long ago the ptarmigan was black like the night. When the dawn came it was too easy for the fox to catch them in the white snow. Many were killed. The ptarmigan went to the wise man and asked for a summer parka the color of tundra and a white parka to blend with the snow. From then on the ptarmigan could be brave thanks to the old man's gift."

Andy looked at his grandfather and said in a small voice, "I wish I had a gift to make me brave."

Tobuk nodded his head slowly. "Maybe there will be such a gift for you," he said and turned away.

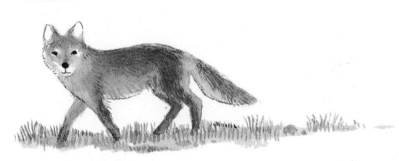

As they climbed toward the top of the ridge the snow became deeper. The sun was a fiery ball sinking in a red sky.

"This is a good spot," said Tobuk. "Plenty of wood for our camp."

"What?!" said Andy. "I thought we would be back by dark."

"No, little one. The sun is almost gone. We'll check traps tomorrow," he said.

Tobuk quickly gathered sticks and laid them crossways for a fire. Soon the flames were crackling and a pot was filled with melting snow. As the old man settled on the ground he called to Andy.

"Here, I have something for you."

The old man's eyes sparkled as he watched Andy pluck the gift from his wrinkled hand. The boy ran his fingers over the smooth surface of the odd shaped bone.

"What is it?" Andy asked.

"It is a piece broken from the tusk of the Woolly Mammoth," Tobuk said.

"The Woolly What!?"

"The Woolly Mammoth," Tobuk repeated as he moved closer to the fire. Andy was also drawn to the flames. As he glanced back into the shadows he shivered. "Tell me about this mammoth, grandfather."

"He was here when the people first came to this great land," Tobuk said. "He was a giant—bigger than three white bears. He had long shaggy hair that hung like the moss in the spruce and tusks the color of the silt in the river. It was long ago when this land was covered with grass as tall as a man."

Andy was amazed. "Was it dark then?" he asked.

"It has always been dark," Tobuk explained. "The night is half of the whole. The moose sleeps during the heat of the day then eats at night. But the hawk needs light to spot the lemmings as they race across the tundra. The world needs both night and day to live and grow."

Later as Andy snuggled into his sleeping bag he wondered at Tobuk's words. He rubbed his hand over the smooth tusk and as the fire died he heard soft snores coming from his grandfather's sleeping bag. He tried to imagine what the mammoth might have looked like but as the night closed around him his old fears came rushing back.

The shadows always played tricks on his eyes. The trees were like monsters and he could imagine strange creatures sliding along the ground. As he peeped out through the fur of his parka ruff there was a strange whistling sound. On the other side of the ridge the howl of the wolves rose like a scream on the wind. Andy clutched the tusk until his knuckles turned white and his heart pounded. He was frozen with fear.

Suddenly something moved in the brush close by and it was like a hundred yellow eyes stared out at him, waiting and angry.

So Andy ran. He ran as fast as he could and still the eyes were close behind him. The ground grabbed at his heels and suddenly he fell, slamming into something huge, and hairy, and alive. Slowly the little boy turned.

As the clouds cleared from the moon he stared up into a pair of brown eyes that glinted in the soft light. A moist, pink trunk snuffed curiously at his mukluks. Andy's fear of the dark was nothing compared to the panic he now felt. His heart seemed as if it would burst from beneath his parka.

The beast's tusks curled back toward the massive shaggy brow that now dipped closer to the small boy. As the long trunk slipped beneath his arms and began to lift him upward Andy held his breath and squeezed his eyes shut.

But nothing happened.

The mammoth just stood quietly, cradling the boy and swinging his head gently back and forth. After a moment, Andy opened one eye. Slowly he reached out with one trembling hand and touched the shaggy head. A low rumble came from the beast as he lifted Andy even higher and deposited him on the soft hair of his back.

It was like a dream looking down on the treetops, warm and safe. Andy looked around in a great circle. The light from the moon winked off the icebergs far out to sea and the air sparkled with crystals.

As the animal lumbered down the ridge, Andy's hand moved along the mammoth's neck, stroking the tangled hair. He wondered why he had ever been afraid of the dark. There was so much to see.

Suddenly there was a rush of sound in the willows and two wolves bounded together, happily rubbing noses in welcome. As they raced ahead toward the river bank the mammoth followed.

It was colder on the river and the ice cracked and groaned. Andy could barely make out the shape of a moose munching on the tender willows. But as he learned to read the shadows on the ground he spotted sharp tracks of the fox and wolverine where they had crept to an open hole for a drink. The air was crisp and Andy could smell the musky scent of the moose mingling with the salt that drifted in from the sea.

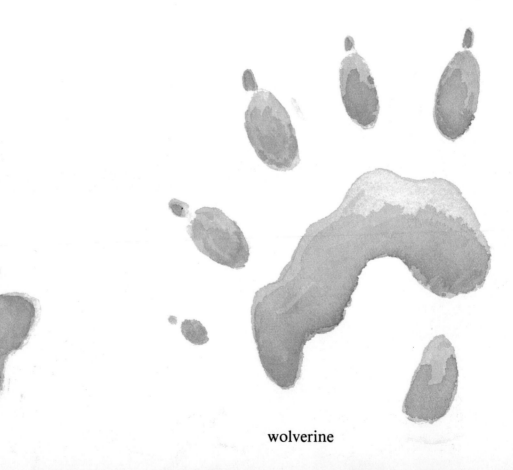

arctic fox   wolverine

The moon now wore a green halo and along the horizon a band of light began to glow. All at once the sky came alive as the Northern Lights shimmered above. The wind was like a song calling his name. "Annn-dy." It sounded like Tobuk. "Ann-dy." As the name whispered through the spruce the mammoth began to shake his head slowly from side to side.

"Andy!"

The shaking grew stronger and suddenly Andy's eyes flew open. "Wake up, sleepy head," Tobuk said. "It's almost dawn."

Andy scrambled from his sleeping bag and rubbed his eyes with his fists. He still held the piece of mammoth tusk and as he looked at his grandfather in wonder, the old man smiled.

"I guess next year you will take the tusk and hunt with your brothers?" Tobuk asked.

"Oh yes," said Andy. "I can hardly wait."

"Good," said Tobuk. "Now run get some wood so we can make breakfast."

"Yes grandfather," Andy said. And as he walked into the shadows to gather wood the little boy was finally at peace with the dark.

THE WOOLLY MAMMOTH

Scientists say the Woolly Mammoth lived in Alaska between 12,000 and 35,000 years ago. They were a part of the elephant family that came over the Bering Land Bridge a half a million years ago.

During those days, known as the Ice Age, there was an ice free corridor in the interior of the state near Fairbanks. But to the north and to the south, near what is now Anchorage, great sheets of glacial ice covered the land.

The Woolly Mammoth is the ancestor of the African and Indian elephants alive today. Alaskan mammoths were about 13 feet tall at the shoulder; much smaller than the Imperial Mammoths that inhabited California.

There were no trees in Alaska then. Instead, the ice free areas were covered with alpine tundra and the animals— bison, horses and the woolly mammoth grazed on lush grasses.

The willow ptarmigan, arctic fox and snowshoe hare also appear in this book.

The End